How to Play the Trumpet

A Beginner's Guide to Learning the Trumpet Basics, Reading Music, and Playing Songs with Audio Recordings

Text Copyright © Lightbulb Publishing

All rights reserved. No part of this guide may be reproduced in any form without permission in writing from the publisher except in the case of brief quotations embodied in critical articles or reviews.

Legal & Disclaimer

The information contained in this book and its contents is not designed to replace or take the place of any form of medical or professional advice; and is not meant to replace the need for independent medical, financial, legal or other professional advice or services, as may be required. The content and information in this book has been provided for educational and entertainment purposes only.

The content and information contained in this book has been compiled from sources deemed reliable, and it is accurate to the best of the Author's knowledge, information, and belief. However, the Author cannot guarantee its accuracy and validity and cannot be held liable for any errors and/or omissions. Further, changes are periodically made to this book as and when needed. Where appropriate and/or necessary, you must consult a professional (including but not limited to your doctor, attorney, financial advisor or such other professional advisor) before using any of the suggested remedies, techniques, or information in this book.

Upon using the contents and information contained in this book, you agree to hold harmless the Author from and against any damages, costs, and expenses, including any legal fees potentially resulting from the application of any of the information provided by this book. This disclaimer applies to any loss, damages or injury caused by the use and application, whether directly or indirectly, of any advice or information presented, whether for breach of contract, tort, negligence, personal injury, criminal intent, or under any other cause of action.

You agree to accept all risks of using the information presented in this book.

You agree that by continuing to read this book, where appropriate and/or necessary, you shall consult a professional (including but not limited to your doctor, attorney, or financial advisor or such other advisor as needed) before using any of the suggested remedies, techniques, or information in this book.

Table of Contents

Chapter 1: Introduction 1

Chapter 2: The Parts, Tuning, and General Care 3

Chapter 3: Selecting the Right Trumpet for You 13

Chapter 4: Understanding Music Notes and Rhythm.................17

Chapter 5: How to Play Notes on the Trumpet..........................27

Chapter 6: Intermediate Trumpet Technique 39

Chapter 7: Examples of Songs to Play.......................................43

Chapter 8: Intermediate Trumpet Techniques............................47

Chapter 9: Bringing it all Together 60

Throughout this book there are musical examples and audio recordings to follow along with on your journey to learn how to play the trumpet.

Whenever you see the following outline:

> **Listening Example #1:** Tuning Notes
>
> Listen to tracks 1.a-1.c
>
> You'll hear what it sounds like for your trumpet to be in tune, flat, and sharp.

Please follow along with the recordings at the Sound Cloud link below or search on Sound Cloud for "How to Play the Trumpet". https://soundcloud.com/jason_randall/sets/how-to-play-the-trumpet

Chapter 1: Introduction

Huzzah! You've decided to pick up the trumpet, congratulations on taking this step! The trumpet is a very vibrant, versatile instrument; it's got a brash reputation but can also be played with silky sensitivity. You can scream like Maynard Ferguson or play it cool like Miles Davis, and it has the power to play not only classical music and jazz but leap over into more modern and mainstream genres like indie rock and electronic music. It's classified as a "brass" instrument, as opposed to the "strings" in your typical orchestra (violin, viola, contrabass, etc.), or the "woodwinds" that sit alongside brass instruments in both big band jazz and concert bands (clarinet, flute, all saxophones, etc.).

The trumpet dates back to 1500 BC; in fact, bronze and silver trumpets can be found in Tutankhamun's grave. These ancient horns didn't have valves or keys, and the earliest models weren't even made of metal; some were ceramic, and some were made of animal horns (like the "shofar," which was mentioned in the Bible). Improvements in metallurgy made the trumpet more useful and the instrument gained demand during the middle ages, Renaissance era, Baroque period and Romantic era. However, all of these trumpets were "natural trumpets," still without any valves or keys to change pitch, thus making all the available notes within a single overtone series (like the bugle, which is still in use today). This limitation kept the trumpet in the shadows as a supporting player for centuries. Then, after decades of countless horn players trying to crack valve technology, Heinrich Stölzel finally figured out how to redirect a player's flow of air through the trumpet into extra tubing with his Stölzel valve in 1815; this lowered the pitch when the valves were depressed, and added to the trumpet's capabilities. François Périnet later perfected the technology in 1838 (and patented it in 1839), and his design is in use on pretty much all standard, valve instruments to this day.

This makes the modern, valve trumpet a relatively new instrument. Its popularity really exploded in the 20th century through jazz; the list of game-changing players at the time is far too long to regurgitate here, but Louis Armstrong and Dizzy Gillespie are a couple of the earliest virtuosos to really invigorate the horn in the public eye. Armstrong also was one of the first to signal the shift in popularity from the slightly smaller cornet (previously the instrument of choice in classical circles) to the more common trumpet we see today, which ended up being ubiquitous in jazz circles.

In addition to the cornet, there are multiple other variations of the trumpet (which we'll get to later), but you'll most likely start with the standard B♭ trumpet. This means when you play a "C" on the trumpet, it will sound like a B♭ on a piano (again, more on this later). So, let's get into what these curved tubes can do for you!

Chapter 2: The Parts, Tuning, and General Care

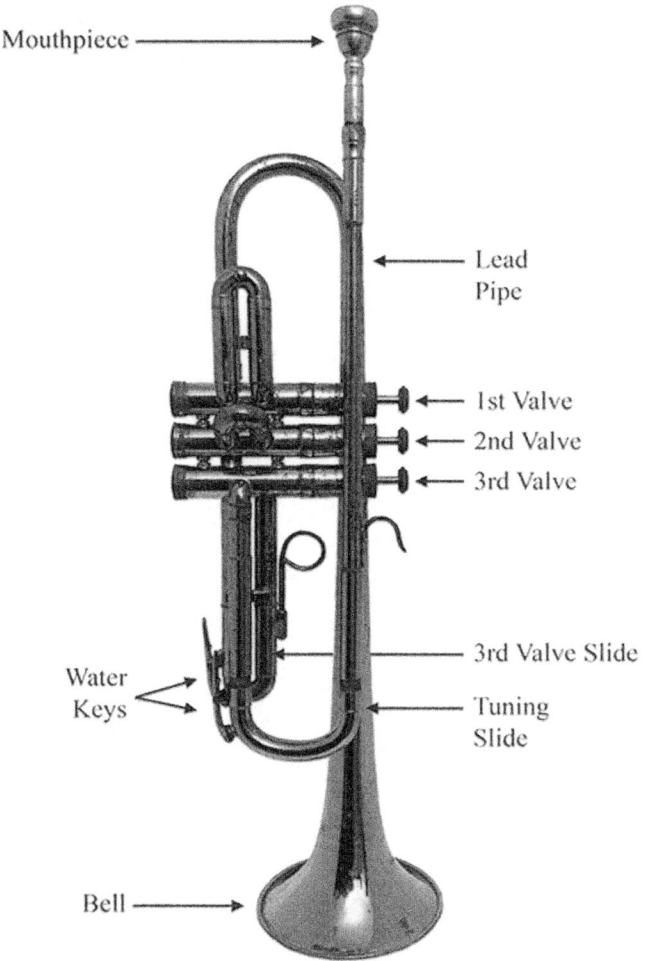

Parts

There are many parts to the trumpet, but they're not all of equal importance. So, let's start with one of the most essential ones. First, the mouthpiece.

As you might've guessed, that's going to be the point of contact between your mouth and the trumpet. To put the mouthpiece into the trumpet, simply hold the trumpet upright and drop the mouthpiece into its designated hole, sometimes called the "mouthpiece receiver." Resist the urge to pound the mouthpiece into the horn with the palm of your hand, as that is likely to get it permanently stuck; the mouthpiece will stay in on its own.

This mouthpiece receiver connects to the "lead pipe" (or "mouth pipe"), which refers to the main tubing that stretches from the mouthpiece holder to the main "tuning slide" of the instrument. This "tuning slide" can be pulled out or pushed in to make slight changes to your horn's pitch. On the bottom of this tuning slide, there is "the water key" (more commonly called a "spit valve").

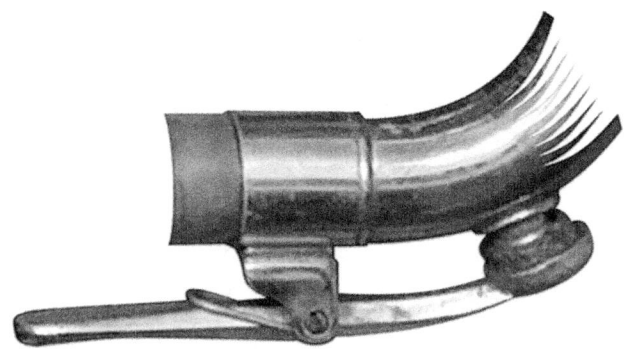

The water key/spit valve opens up to release trapped condensation (not spit) from the inside of the tuning slide. You'll know you need to use it when your horn makes a "gargling" noise instead of clean tones. You can do this by opening the water key, blowing through the horn, and then semi-randomly pushing down and releasing all of your pistons (to clear the condensation out of the valves). Do this over a spare, unimportant rag.

Continuing along the tubing; next, we have the valves. Inside the valves are "pistons," just like those on a car. When you push down on any of the three "buttons" in the middle of the horn, they will activate these pistons which are mostly made of metal but have holes in them. As the pistons descend, these holes will align with the valve slide tubes and redirect the air flowing through the horn into these valve slides.

Notice how the second valve slide is the shortest, the first valve slide is longer, and the third valve slide is the longest. These pistons are set in the valves with "valve caps," which screw the pistons onto the top of the valve casings. On most horns, your third valve slide will have its own water key.

Whether you are pressing down on valves or not, your air flow eventually continues up towards the "bell," which is the name of the wide opening at the end of the trumpet. This is also where we can add mutes to your trumpet, which are separate "parts" that any trumpet player should get their hands on.

As the name suggests, mutes can muffle, quiet, or otherwise change the sound of your horn. They come in a few different varieties to achieve different effects, and are used by simply jamming them into the bell of your horn (they stay in place securely and safely through small chunks of cork that are glued onto the mute, so as to also not harm the inside of your trumpet).

These mutes not only come in different shapes, but can also be made of a few different materials, thus adding more variety.

The most neutral shape, or model of mute is the "straight mute," which is intended to have no effect on the trumpet's sound, save for making it quieter. It's generally just a cone shape, and when it's made of metal, can add a slight "buzzy-ness" to the sound, especially when the horn is played loudly; however, models like the Humes and Berg "stonelined" straight mute leave the sound less affected.

The second most common mute (and arguably second-most neutral) is the "cup mute." It's constructed just like a straight mute, but with an extra, bowl-like piece that adds a bit more character to the sound. However, this pales in comparison to the "Harmon" (or "wah-wah") mute, which thoroughly affects the sound. This mute will give your horn an extra "buzzy" tone, and comes with a removable "stem" (which looks like an oversized mouthpiece) for two different sounds. Miles Davis famously used this mute on his Kind of Blue record.

Tuning

Tuning is actually a bit more advanced, so don't worry about it for the time being. Come back to this paragraph when you can hold a consistent, even pitch for long periods of time (you might finish the rest of the book before then, which is totally fine, we'll wait)...

OKAY! So now that you can do this, get someone (who can find it) to play the Bb right under middle C on the piano and hold it. At the same time, play a long, solid, low C. As you train your ears through "centering" your notes (more on that later), we'll also be able to tell whether you are "sharp," (all of your notes are slightly too high) "flat," (the opposite) or "in tune" (right on target). When your notes are centered and played as naturally as possible, if they still sound just a bit off, adjust your tuning slide and retry. If you are too "flat," pull in your tuning slide just a touch - if you are too "sharp," pull it out.

We tend to want our tuning slide, on average, pulled out about a half of an inch. It's good to push it all the way back in when the horn isn't in use to avoid the slide from getting dried out, but we never want to actually *play* with the slide pushed all the way in. If you think about it, that's the "sharpest," or highest in pitch, that the trumpet will go. So, you'll likely never want to play your horn without your tuning slide out a bit. But again, this is all a bit more advanced, so let's get into trumpet maintenance.

> **Listening Example #1:** Tuning Notes
>
> Listen to tracks 1.a-1.c
>
> You'll hear what it sounds like for your trumpet to be in tune, flat, and sharp.

Care

There are a few essential pieces of trumpet maintenance equipment that should come with every horn; if you get your horn used, make sure you get ahold of these products:

- Valve Oil
- Slide Grease
- Cleaning Snake
- Mouthpiece Brush
- Trumpet Cloth (optional)
- Valve Guard (optional)

Let's discuss what each piece is for. The slide grease is for all of your slides - your main tuning slide, the first valve slide, the third valve slide, and the second valve "slide" (the one that's so tiny it's misleading to call it a slide, but that's its name so we'll run with it). Pull all of your slides out, and coat the parts of these slides that are normally inside the slide casings with slide grease. It'll give these slides a very viscous, syrupy-slow movement, like they're swimming in molasses. But, they won't get stuck! Then, we will dilute the grease with a bunch of valve oil to make these slides move more quickly. The tuning slide doesn't really need to move quickly, but our first and third valve slides will need to be fast. We'll touch on that later.

The valve oil is also needed exactly where you'd expect it: inside the valves. Before you ever try playing your horn, twist the valve caps counter-clockwise to remove the pistons from the valve casings one at a time. Pour a generous amount of valve oil on the side of each piston, then screw them back in. Anytime your pistons get sticky in your valves, repeat this process to lubricate them and improve their functioning. If the problem persists, you may need to clean the caps on the bottom of the valves. If the side surfaces of the pistons wear down, they will get stuck regularly no matter what and need to be refinished. Hopefully it doesn't come to that, though!

Valve Oil

The cleaning snake and mouthpiece cleaner are really just glorified pipe cleaners designed for trumpet. The main cleaning snake will work for the lead pipe and tuning slide - first, remove your tuning slide and run the snake from the lead pipe through to where the tuning slide *would* plug in. Then, try running the snake through the tuning slide itself. The bristles on the snake will rub out the grime that builds inside your horn, and they're coated to protect the inside of your trumpet as well.

Cleaning Snake

Similarly, use the mouthpiece cleaner the same way - dig into the bottom part (or output) of the mouthpiece with the pointed end of the bristles and twist the mouthpiece cleaner around. Then remove it - you've now cleaned your mouthpiece!

Here are some optional accoutrements: the trumpet cloth and valve guard. Trumpet cloths are coated very lightly in a polishing solution, which will rub off finger oils and give your horn a pristine shine. They often come in different varieties for horns of different colors (e.g. silver vs brass/gold). Resist the urge to use this polishing rag to catch condensation out of your water key! Lastly, a valve guard is an optional accessory you can buy which wraps around the valves and protects your valve casings from the oil on your fingers. It may seem unnecessary at first, but the longer you keep your horn and the more often you play it, the more corrosion will affect the finish on the valve casings!

Now that you know how to care for your horn, what should we look for when buying or renting?

Chapter 3: Selecting the Right Trumpet for You

If you're just starting out, it's probably best to make sure you get a standard, B♭ trumpet. The fact that it's called a "B♭ trumpet" means that when you play a C on the trumpet, you're actually playing the same pitch as a B♭ on a piano (or in "concert pitch"). The B♭ trumpet is transposed one step off from concert pitch - you can buy a "C trumpet," which makes your trumpet's C match the C on a piano. But most sheet music you'll encounter will accommodate this transposition as the B♭ trumpet is more traditional.

Other variations on the trumpet include the cornet and the flugelhorn. Cornets are smaller and "brighter"-sounding than trumpets. Flugelhorns go in the opposite direction, slightly larger and "warmer"-sounding than trumpets. Again, if you're going for the best all-around point of entry, the standard B♭ trumpet is the best choice. Unless extreme portability is an issue, in which case you can go for the extra-small, extra-bright "pocket trumpet," which is so short that its case is nearly cubic.

Then there's the issue of *which* trumpet to rent or buy. Honestly, people get way too hung up on equipment - on all instruments. Far too many musicians think they'll make a major breakthrough in their technical abilities and talent by upgrading their gear. While a superior horn will cause less air resistance, have a more pleasant tone, and simply be more aesthetically pleasing, it won't turn you into Miles Davis overnight; on that note, a great musician can make any horn sing. In fact, I've got a no-name, beaten-up and nearly-broken horn that was donated to me a couple years ago. For the past year or so, I've enjoyed playing it over my $3,000+ professional horn (I'm not going to name names here, though).

It's fine to rent, and it's fine to buy used. Just make sure the horn doesn't have too much corrosion around the valves where finger oils may have wreaked havoc. Also, if the pistons are regularly getting stuck in the valves even after oiling the pistons and cleaning out the inside of the valves and valve caps, that can be a red flag for future issues. Since you need to have the horn for a while to see how regular of a problem this is, it's good to rent a horn or buy it with a longer return policy. Which horn you pick, especially when starting, isn't that important - just get a trumpet within your budget that you can repair for free or return if it breaks.

Perhaps of even bigger importance is selecting the right mouthpiece. Again, different trumpets will have different timbres, levels of "brightness" or "warmth" to their tone. Some will be more versatile than others, or easier to play, or sound less "tinny." But the mouthpiece is like sticks to a drummer - it's the way you connect your body to your instrument. To continue the analogy: it's better to play on a crappy drum set with the right sticks for both your hands and the gig than to play on a beautiful, priceless kit with sticks that either snap after one song, or massively overpower the coffee shop jazz trio you're gigging with. Similarly, mouthpieces come in different sizes for different purposes.

To further confuse things, different companies use different numbering systems for their mouthpiece sizes. It's probably best to snag a size Bach 7C mouthpiece when you're first starting out. If you get a student trumpet, this is likely the mouthpiece that came with it. For a slightly fuller, fatter sound, you can get a Bach 3C, or even a 1 1/2 C (the decreasing numbers make the cup size bigger, and the ability to get a pleasant tone easier, although you might sacrifice some of your range). Once you're well beyond this book, it might be time to explore mouthpieces that aid in getting high notes like the Schilke 14A4A (although then you sacrifice tone and "warmth").

Your local music store should have plenty of options for both renting and buying, and OfferUp/Craigslist are also fine places to shop for your first (used) horn. Just like buying a used car, though, you might want to find a local repair shop that you trust as well. If you do decide to rent or buy new, go to the local music shop that has brass or woodwind instruments! These stores are getting harder to find, so if you want them to continue existing, patronize them!

Chapter 4: Understanding Music Notes and Rhythm

You may be tempted to just "play the dang thing already," and we're almost there! But first, we need to understand how to read sheet music, so that we can learn the pitches and rhythms that make up the notes we play. The trumpet, like all wind instruments, is "monophonic," meaning it can only play one note at a time (save for some special-effects musicians). Notes have two components - "pitch" and "rhythm."

Pitch

"Pitch" is fairly self-explanatory - it determines the tone of a note, how "high" or "low" it sounds. We name our different pitches with letters from A to G (where we restart). For instance, the first pitch most trumpet players learn is a "low C." What pitch a note holds can be determined by how high or low the note is on the staff.

All of our pitches will be displayed on a music staff, but not all music staffs are the same. Our music staff is graced with what's called the "treble clef," and this name dictates the "treble" range the trumpet plays in (as opposed to the lower "bass clef"). Think "All about that bass / no treble" from Meghan Trainor's song, if that helps - we're in a higher range than those low bass instruments, but not crazy high in the sky.

As a beginner trumpet player, it will be hard for you to hit very many pitches right out of the gate, due to the huge demands of your lungs, lips, etc. For instance, a beginner pianist needs to learn many notes immediately (since they only need to move their fingers -

literally anyone can play any note on the piano, but the trumpet is not so forgiving). So, it's pretty common to just memorize the first several pitches by rote without a mnemonic. Still, here's a couple weird tricks that I've enjoyed to keep track of these pitches; some are conventional, some just come from a quirky, alternative perspective.

Low C - often the first note beginners can play - is below the main treble clef staff, but has a line through it. Between the note's importance and unique look, it might end up one of the easier ones to remember.

D and E - if you've got low C pretty well memorized, you can figure out both of these notes by simply counting how much higher each one of them sits above low C (just remember to include lines *and* spaces as you go up the staff). D sits on the space just below the staff, while E sits on the staff's bottom line. However, we can't count up from low C as we're playing, we need to just know our pitches. One strange tip to keep these separated is the fact that the letter D does not have a line through the middle of it (just like the note D, which sits on a space). However, the letter E *does* have a line sticking through the middle of it, like the note. That might be more confusing than helpful, depending on how your brain works, but that's up to you (if it's just confusing - see EGBDF rule ahead).

F - see: "FACE" rule (ahead).

G - the "treble clef" is also called "the G-clef." Not only does the treble clef look somewhat like a capital "G" in a very weird, Walt Disney-esque font (if you use your imagination), but it also loops around the second-from-bottom line of the staff. It almost looks like crosshairs. This second line of the staff is where the G sits that gives the "G-clef" it's name (also see: EGBDF rule ahead).

For higher notes, the typical mnemonic tricks for learning the staff include the word "FACE" and one of these variations: "**E**very **G**ood **B**urger **D**eserves **F**ries," "**E**very **G**ood **B**oy **D**oes **F**ine," "**E**very **G**ood **B**oy **D**eserves **F**udge," etc. "FACE" spells out the pitch letters of all the spaces inside the staff, while the "EGBDF" sayings spell out the pitch letters of the notes on all of the staff's lines.

F   A   C   E

Before we move onto rhythms, let's add "accidentals" to our note repertoire. In case you're unfamiliar with what pitches look like on a piano, here's a quick refresher:

Notice how we don't have names for any of the black keys? That's where "accidentals" come in. (Side-bar: feel free to gloss over, skim, or simply ignore this section for as you don't need this information until later - come back after you've played through the basic songs mentioned in chapter 7).

"Accidentals" are an umbrella terms for three pitch-shifting symbols: the "sharp" (♯), the "flat" (♭), and the "natural" (♮). "Sharps" raise a note's pitch up the smallest distance we can move in Western music: what we're going to call a "half-step." This usually turns a note that would be a "white key" on a piano into a "black key" (but not always). "Flats" do the opposite by pushing a note down (or "flattening" it) a half-step. So, these in-between, black-key-on-a-piano notes actually go by two names. For instance, C♯ is the same note as D♭ - you can raise C up one half-step, or take D down a half-step, and either way you end up in the same spot. All of these accidentals continue for the entire measure. So, if you see a G♯ in the beginning of a measure, and another G later in the same measure (on the same line), it will also be played as a G♯. If the composer wants you to play a normal G, they'll need to use the "natural," as the natural symbol cancels out sharps and flats. That's why a normal G pitch can also be called a "G-natural." However, should you encounter a mid-range G♯ near the beginning of a measure and a *high* G later in the same measure, this "accidentals last for the whole measure" rule won't apply; the high G will be played as a "G-natural."

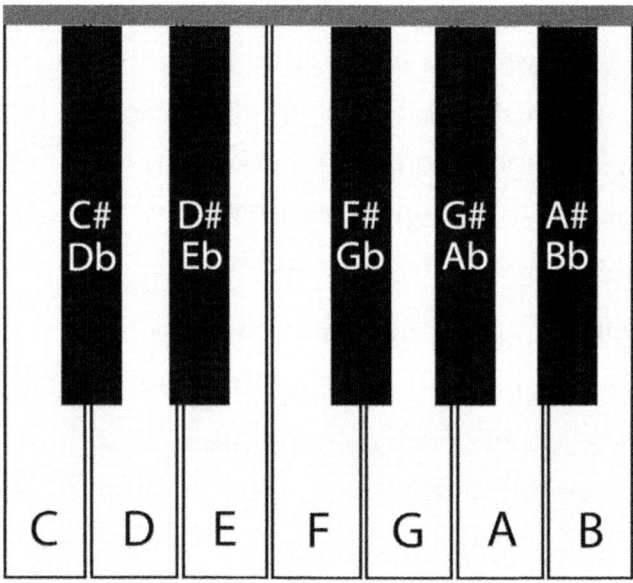

Eventually, you'll encounter "key signatures," which will tell you at the beginning of a song to flat or sharp all notes of a certain pitch (in *any* octave or range) for the entire song unless otherwise noted with a natural. For instance, in this key, you'll need to turn every F you see into an F♯ unless the note is specifically equipped with a natural.

Again, this is all information you'll need later, but for now we're just getting into the weeds. Let's move on and get ready to groove!

Rhythm

"Rhythm" helps us differentiate the *timing* and *duration* of notes. These different "rhythms" are based around what's called the "beat" (or the "pulse") of a song. That's the speed your toe naturally wants to tap along to when listening to a song (or your head naturally wants to bob at). Whether you love, hate, or are nostalgic for dance tracks like "Uptown Funk" by Mark Ronson and Bruno Mars, or "Gangnam Style" by PSY, they're great tracks to "feel the beat" on. There's a kick drum on every beat, and you just want to move your body along with it (even begrudgingly).

This "beat" is denoted with what is called a "quarter note," which looks like this ♩. Note the black/filled-in circle and the line (or "stem") protruding from it. Notes that look like this are played at the same speed as "the beat," or the "pulse" of a song.

Other note rhythms will take different shapes. For instance, the "half note" lasts for *two* beats. So, if you're tapping your toe along to pulse of a song, simply hold the note for two of these toe taps. Notice that half notes look like quarter notes, but the main note head is "hollow," or white. Similarly, "whole notes" last for *four* beats and also use a hollow or white note head, but the stem is gone completely.

Putting a "dot" to the side of the note head makes one-and-a-half times as long as it normally would be. The only one of these that you'll see in the immediate future is the "dotted half note," which lasts for *three* beats (since normal half notes are two, you'd add one extra beat as that is half the length of the original note).

Note that the "dot" is to the side of the note head opposite the stem, not above or below the head, as that means something different (and we don't need to get into here). You can also add a "dot" to other rhythms, but again, let's save that for another time.

Almost done! We just need to add notes that are *faster* than a quarter note. There are many variations, but will just mention one of them: "eighth notes," which are exactly twice as fast as quarter notes. Or, if you prefer to think of it this way, each eighth note lasts for one half of a beat.

These names are based on the fraction each note takes up of what is called a "measure," which typically is **four beats long** (at least if the song is in 4/4, as many are). These "measures," or "bars," are the boxes our notes sit in; the vertical lines on our music staff denote the beginnings and endings of measures.

(each space between the vertical lines represents one "measure," or bar)

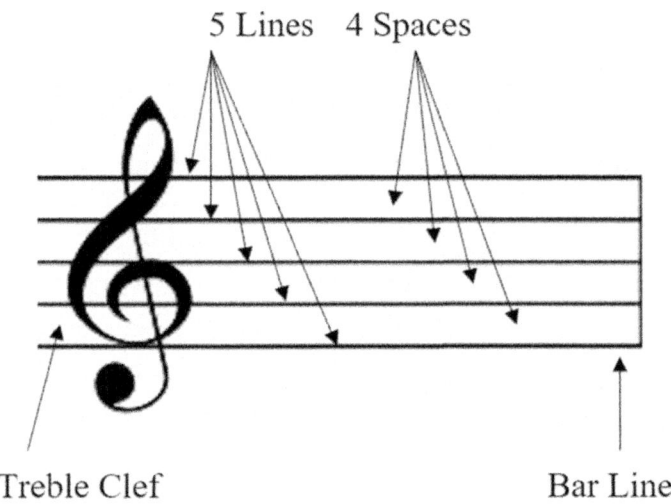

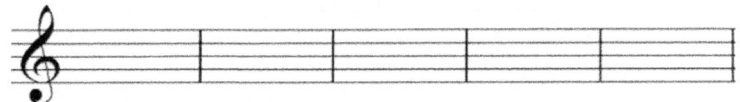

Lastly: for each of these rhythms, there is not only a "note," but also a "rest." So, if a quarter note lasts for one beat, so does a quarter rest. However, as the name implies, a rest means that you don't play for the same duration as the corresponding note. A "half rest" means you would rest for two beats, just like a half note, and a "whole rest" means you'd rest for four beats, just as you would play a whole note for the same amount of time:

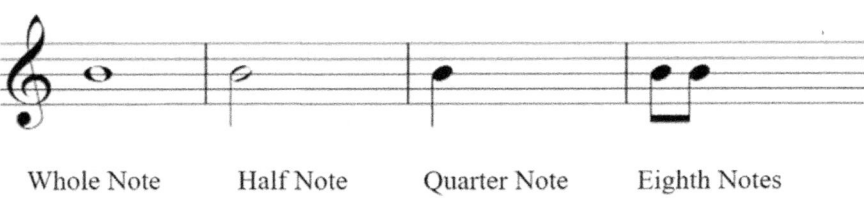

Whole Note   Half Note   Quarter Note   Eighth Notes

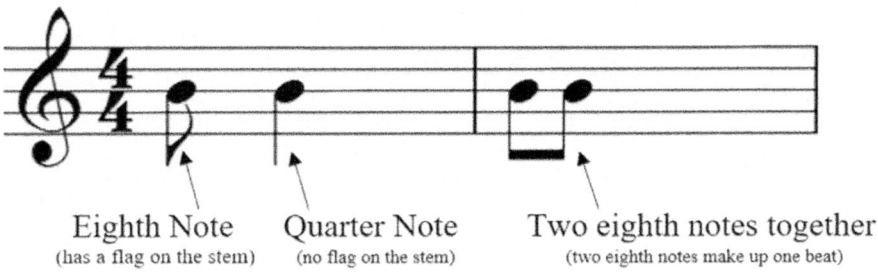

Eighth Note   Quarter Note   Two eighth notes together
(has a flag on the stem) (no flag on the stem) (two eighth notes make up one beat)

How to Play the Trumpet

Whole Note = 4 Beats

Half Note = 2 Beats

Quarter Note = 1 Beat

Eighth Note = ½ Beat

Whole Rest   Half Rest   Quarter Rest

Whole Rest = 4 Beats

Half Rest = 2 Beats

Quarter Rest = 1 Beat

Chapter 5: How to Play Notes on the Trumpet

Getting Your Setup

Alright, we're ready to start playing! Let's make sure your embouchure, posture, and your overall setup are on point. Some of these concepts will even be reusable for other, non-wind instruments, too!

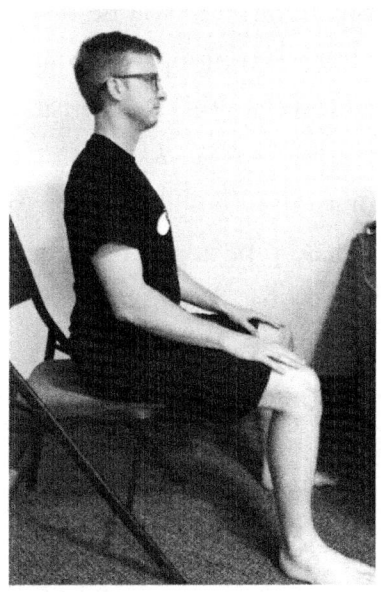

First off, sit up straight on the edge of your seat. However, don't arch your back *backwards* as students often do - any curvature of your spine forwards *or* backwards will cut off airflow. Just point your torso straight upward while keeping every part of your body relaxed. Let's now pick up the horn.

Hold the horn by the valves with your left hand. This hand will do all the lifting, while your right hand will do all of the playing and *zero* lifting of the trumpet. Wrap your left hand's fingers around the valves of the horn in a very intuitive fashion; your thumb will wrap around the first valve towards your body, while all of your other fingers will wrap around the third valve on the other side. If your first valve has a "finger ring," "thumb hook," or "thumb saddle," go ahead and put your left thumb in there. You'll almost definitely have a "finger ring" on your third valve slide; you'll want to put your left hand's ring finger in there. Keep all of your other fingers below the lead pipe.

The fingers on your right hand will be responsible for activating the pistons, so you will be setting up your right hand for maximum ergonomic efficiency. However, this is surprisingly not quite intuitive. First, dig your right thumb *in between the first and second valves*, right under the lead pipe. Your first impulse will probably be to stick your right thumb in between the lead pipe and other main tubing that leads up to the bell, but opt instead for that nook between first valve casing, second valve casing, and the lead pipe (we'll explain in a bit). Another thing you'll be tempted to do is stick your right pinky finger into the "pinky ring" aka "finger ring" that sits atop the lead pipe. Instead, please your pinky finger on top of the pinky ring. Here's why:

Wrapping your thumb around the lead pipe decreases your ability to activate the pistons with your finger*tips* in a purely vertical fashion. It forces the palm of your hand in too close to the trumpet. This forces you to only be able to push down on the pistons with second-knuckle part of your fingers instead of using your actual fingertips and getting more leverage from the rest of your fingers. You'll also end up slightly pushing sideways on the pistons, causing them to get stuck in the valves far more often.

As for your right hand - here's why we avoid using the pinky ring. Our ring finger is stupid, uncoordinated and codependent. It doesn't know how to function on its own, and desperately tries to drag both the middle and *especially* pinky fingers along on its adventures. So, looking up our pinky finger in this ring hampers our ring finger's dexterity. So, by simply placing the pinky finger *atop* the ring, it's free to move wherever it wants, so we won't limit the mobility of the ring finger on the third valve's piston.

Next, we need to tackle our "embouchure." "Embouchure" is a kind of umbrella term for the entire setup your teeth, lips, and facial muscles will form as you play your horn. The specifics of a perfect embouchure are often a topic of debate between players of even world-class talent. This general approach is fairly universal:

- Start by pronouncing the letter "M".
- Then, "flex" or "pull back" the corners of your mouth very tightly
- But, don't let your lips roll over each other nor around the edge of your teeth
- Finally, blow air through your lips

Some trumpeters use this analogy: "pretend you're about to blow on some hot soup to try to cool it." However, we will eventually pull back our lips more tightly than we would to cool soup. This tightness of the lips will affect how "buzzy" the sound is that comes out of your lips as the air passes through.

As you try for your first note, remember one last thing. Say "tah!" into the mouthpiece as you play each note; this is called "tonguing." Until we master the concept of "slurring," it's good to tongue every note so we don't get into the habit of "hah-ing" our notes - this is a terrible habit that is very hard to break. Slurring involves us eventually going between different notes without tonguing, but just changing notes by using different valve pistons and/or changing wind speeds. Even then, we don't want to exhale inconsistently in a "hah"-like manner. We want to play with a steady stream of air and separate our notes with a "Tah!" inside our mouth, as the front tip of your tongue hits the roof of your mouth (more on that later). So let's try it! Blow a consistent stream of air into the horn as you hit the roof of your mouth with your tongue (like you're saying "Tah" into your trumpet).

> **Listening Example #2:** Tah Tonguing
>
> Listen to tracks 2.a-2.b

Down the line, we can even start to utilize "double" or even "triple" tonguing. All of these techniques are advanced, so either come back to this paragraph later when single tonguing is mastered and you've played for a few years! Normal, or "single" tonguing employs a "tah" sound by hitting the roof of your mouth with the tip of your tongue, but we can increase the speed of our tonguing by also utilizing a "kah" sound (produced with the *back* of the tongue hitting the roof of the mouth). It's a clumsy approach that doesn't sound very good when played by itself or at slower speeds, but alternating between "tah" and "kah" tonguing works very well at faster speeds where single tonguing is unsustainable. "Triple tonguing" is really just a repeating, three-note combination of these two tonguing styles, meant for use on fast triplets - the combinations include "Tah-ka-tah" and "Tah-tak-kah," the first of which is my personal go-to.

> **Listening Example #3:** Triple/Double Tonguing
> in Low C
>
> Listen to tracks 3.a-3.c

Multiple factors will affect how high or low your notes come out as you play them. Namely, the speed at which you blow air through your lips, how tightly-pulled-back your lips are over your teeth (or how tightly-pulled-back the corners of your mouth are), and also whether you're "aiming up" or "down" into the mouthpiece (in other words, the angle of your airstream through your mouth into the mouthpiece). The faster the wind speed, the more firm the corners of your mouth are, the more tightly-pressed your lips are, and the higher you aim into the mouthpiece, the higher the notes will come out (and vice versa). Try to keep all of these factors consistent for the duration of the note you're playing.

Changing all of these factors drastically will give you the ability to jump into a different range of notes, even without the use of the pistons. These different ranges are called "partials." For instance, low C and the G on the second line of the staff are both played with a "0" fingering (don't push down on any valves). However, they're played with different wind speeds and intensities. Blow slower air with more relaxed lips for low C, and faster air and tighter lips for G. Eventually, you'll get higher and higher "partials" as you develop the muscles in your embouchure and your lung capacity. This is how different notes were played on the "natural trumpets" and bugles mentioned earlier.

Trumpet Fingering Chart

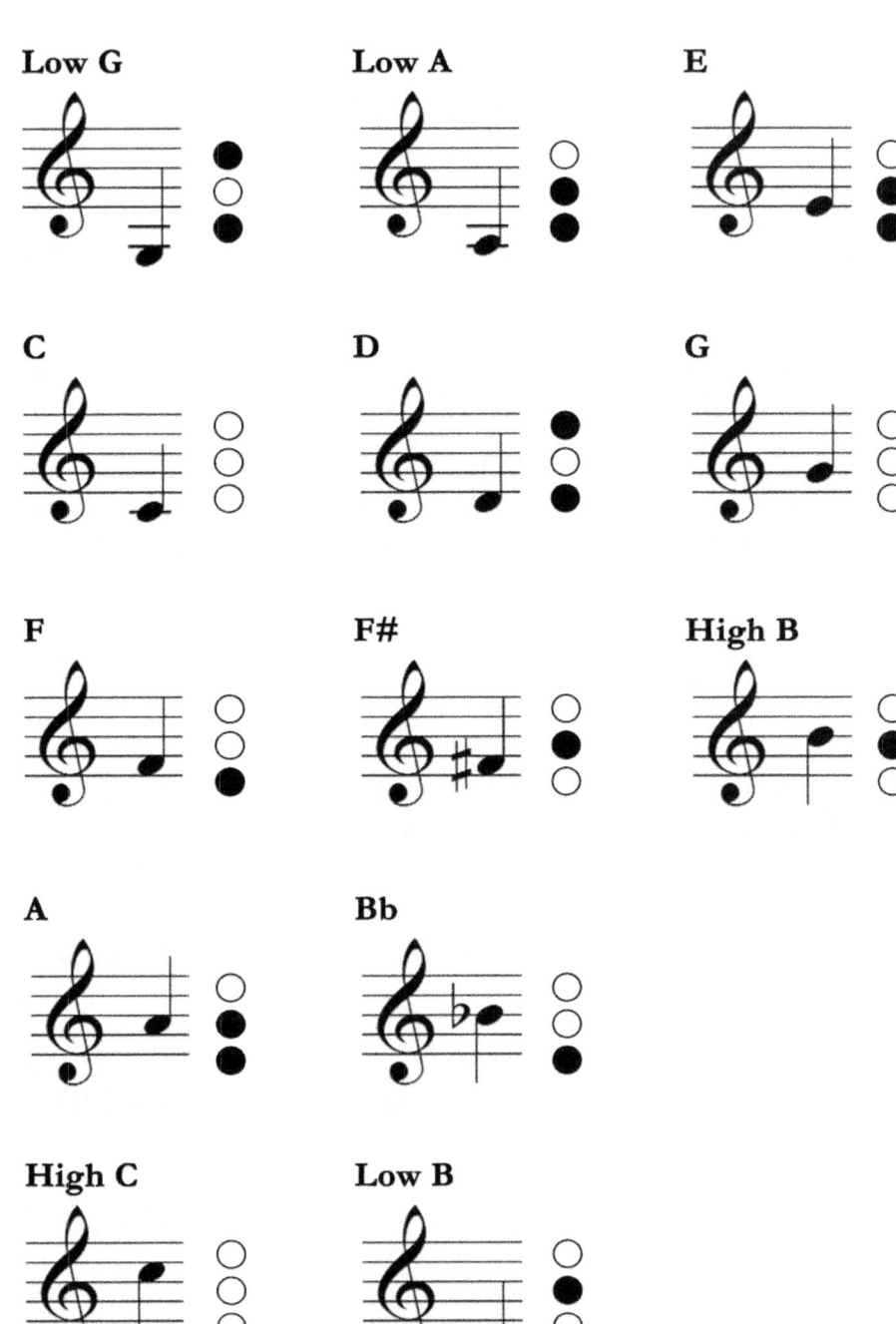

4a: Long Note – A

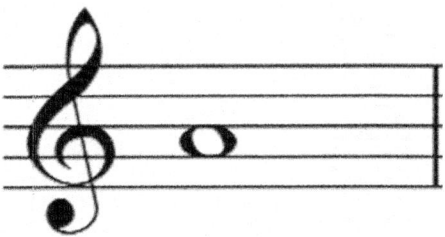

4b: Long Note – A (low)

Listening Example #4: A Notes

Listen to tracks 4.a-4.b

5a: Long Note – B

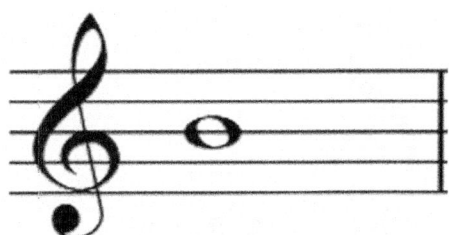

5b: Long Note – B (low)

5c: Long Note – Bb

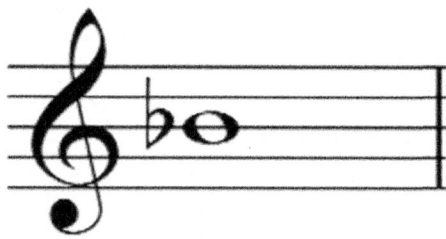

Listening Example #5: B Notes

Listen to tracks 5.a-5.c

6a: Long Note – C

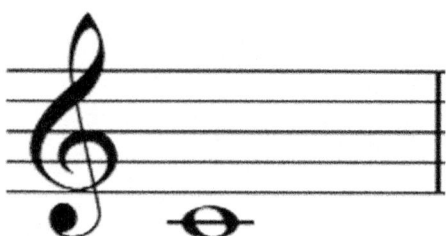

6b: Long Note – C (high)

Listening Example #6: C Notes

Listen to tracks 6.a-6.b

7: Long Note – D

Listening Example #7: D Note

Listen to track 7

8: Long Note – E

```
┌─────────────────────────────────────────┐
│  Listening Example #8: E Note           │
│                                         │
│  Listen to track 8                      │
└─────────────────────────────────────────┘
```

9a: Long Note – F

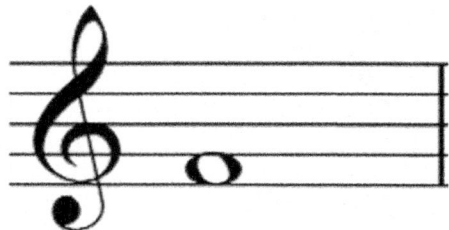

9b: Long Note – F#

> **Listening Example #9:** F Notes
>
> Listen to tracks 9.a-9.b

10a: Long Note – G

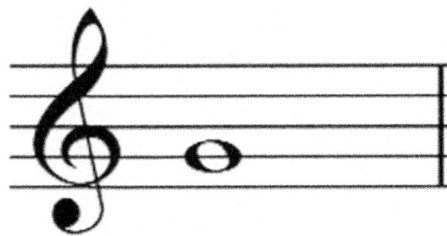

10b: Long Note – G (low)

> **Listening Example #10:** G Notes
>
> Listen to tracks 10.a-10.b

Chapter 6: Intermediate Trumpet Technique

Here, we'll cover some overall trumpet-specific tips:

Breathing

- Always be breathing in or blowing out air! In other words, never "hold your breath." To help make this happen, only breathe in on the last beat of a count-in before starting to play. If you breathe in at the wrong time, simply let it out, re-count into the song, and try to get it at the right time on the second go.

- Over time, try to get good at using all of your breath each time you inhale; don't keeping breathing in out of fear that you'll run out of air when you haven't used all of your air. If you do, you'll end up with leftover, "stale" air (CO_2) in your lungs that's unusable. Countless beginner students of mine have to exhale as they finish a phrase because of all this stale air.

- Your breathing should sound somewhat like Darth Vader, or like a spooky gust of wind. It should be deep, and through your mouth, which will be in an "O" shape. If done right, it'll tickle the back of your throat and make you want to yawn. You'll activate your diaphragm, and your belly will jump out before your shoulders or chest move at all. Speaking of shoulders and chest...

Some Don'ts

- Don't let your shoulders come up before playing. That's a crutch that trumpeters often use to get higher notes (but lower quality notes) by actually cutting off our own air supply. The same goes for elbowing yourself in the ribs.

- Don't puff your cheeks. Basically, all I can say is just focus on not letting the air in. You want to be making a Professor McGonagall face when you play (stern, flat lips pulled back over teeth, like you're about to tell someone how disappointed you are in them):

Some Do's

- Try to think of your wind supply as a steady stream, and the beginnings of notes are just slight separations of that stream with your tongue (or your fingers changing the pitch/note without even using your tongue, if you are slurring). It's like your stream of air is a garden hose with the water turned on, and your tonguing and notes are quick glides of your finger across the hose's stream of water. This one will be harder to do until you've mastered diaphragm breathing, though.

- Do try to open your throat when you're playing and breathing - you can practice it by trying to make a cartoonish "big/strong/manly-man" voice, and then recreate how that feels inside your throat before breathing and playing. Your throat will be open and the back of your tongue won't be obstructing the air-flow (we only want to use the front tip of our tongue when tonguing, while the back remains glued to the bottom of your mouth - almost like you're gagging).

- As an added bit of intermediate technique: low D's and C#'s are notoriously *always* sharp compared to the rest of your range (whatever that may be). On quick notes like quarter and eighth notes, it's not too noticeable. However, on longer notes, the poor intonation may even distract you; you might think you're playing a wrong note even when you're not. Kick out your third valve slide (or possibly first, if you prefer) on these notes to avoid the intonation issues. That's why we make sure these slides are greased *and* very well-oiled.

Chapter 7: Examples of Songs to Play

Now that we've got some notes down, let's form them into songs! Although, first we should start by playing whole notes on one pitch at a time, followed by whole rests. So, we'll start by playing a low C for four toe taps at a very average-to-slow speed, followed by four beats of rest at the same speed. Once we can maintain these C's consistently for the whole measure, we'll move on to D, then E, then F, and G if we can. If notes start to crack or you aren't able to sustain them for the full measure with a consistent stream of air or sound, then bail on that pitch and stick to the ones you can hit solidly. Then, we'll pick songs to play based on your range.

Most of the first songs you'll tackle require three notes to play: C, D, and E. Some great starter songs with these include:

Hot Cross Buns (120 bpm)

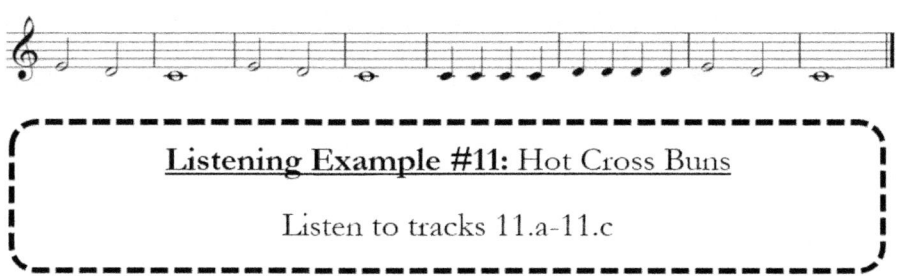

> **Listening Example #11:** Hot Cross Buns
>
> Listen to tracks 11.a-11.c

Mary Had a Little Lamb (120 bpm – no G)
(Simplified Version)

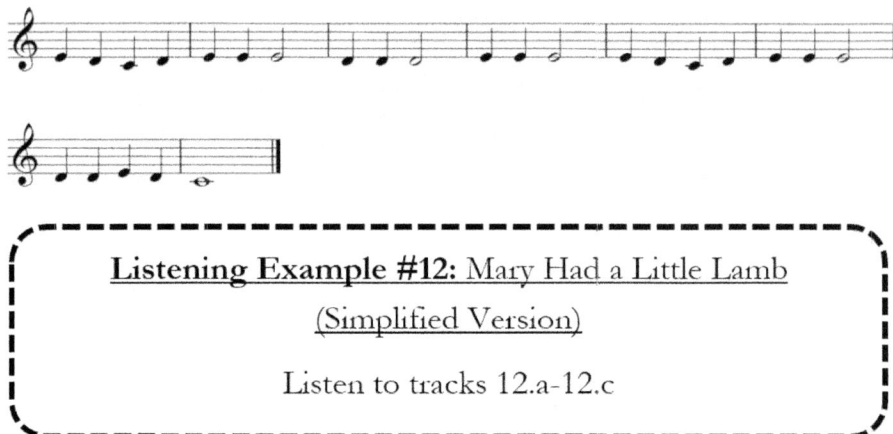

Listening Example #12: Mary Had a Little Lamb (Simplified Version)

Listen to tracks 12.a-12.c

After that, we can add that some more songs that include notes all the way up to G (so C, D, E, F, and G, and A if noted):

Mary Had a Little Lamb (120 bpm) (Slightly Harder Version)

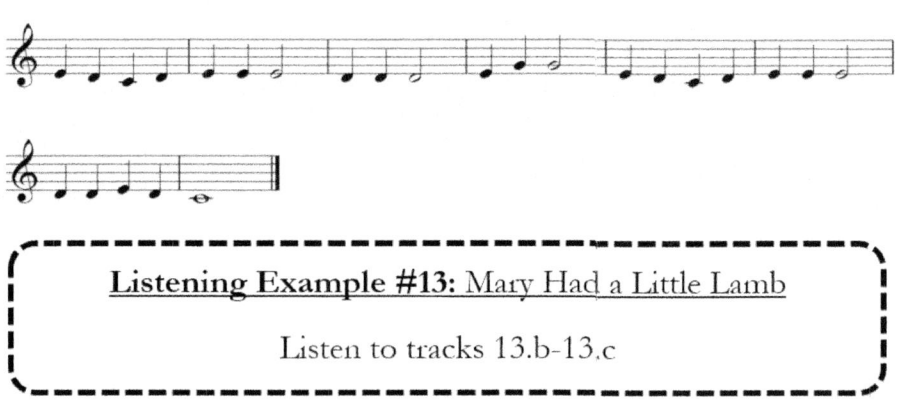

Listening Example #13: Mary Had a Little Lamb

Listen to tracks 13.b-13.c

Frere Jacques (120 bpm) (this one goes all the way up to A, just briefly)

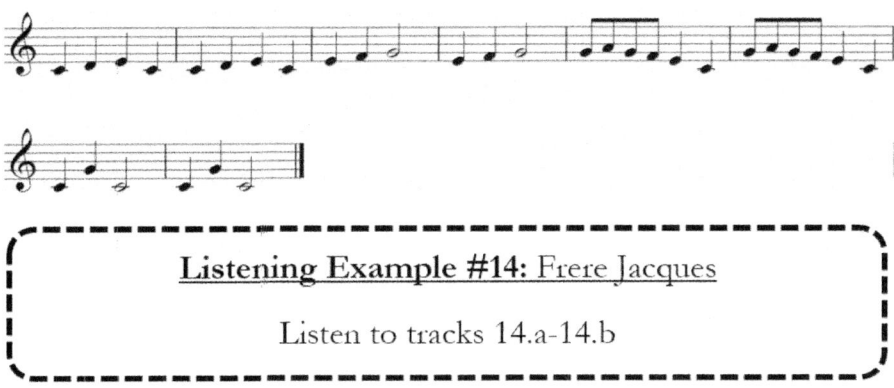

> **Listening Example #14:** Frere Jacques
>
> Listen to tracks 14.a-14.b

Jingle Bells Chorus (slightly simplified rhythm for beginners) (chorus only)

> **Listening Example #15:** Jingle Bells
>
> Listen to track 15

Twinkle Twinkle (120 bpm) (or the ABCs song, as they are the same exact melody - this one also briefly hits A)

Listening Example #16: Twinkle, Twinkle, Little Star

Listen to tracks 16.b-16.c

There are educational books (which we'll mention in the next chapter) that include all of these songs and more, gradually increasing the difficulty and range of these songs to stretch out your abilities. But, there are also pieces of sheet music that you can find online and buy individually 'a la carte' that might pique your fancy. These pieces are transcribed from popular Top 40 hits, movie soundtracks, and the like; they're usually transcribed in either the recording's original key or the closest-to-original key that is beginner-to-intermediate level appropriate. Often, these sites offer transposition to whichever key you'd like, and the transcriptions are generally quite accurate! These sites include MusicNotes.com, SheetMusicPlus.com, SheetMusicDirect.com, SheetMusicNow.com, MuseScore.com, etc. Some of them utilize freelancers to do transcriptions, while others combine these freelancers with crowd-sourcing of the site's users of the site (like MuseScore.com); the latter will have a bigger repertoire but be less accurate on the whole than sites like SheetMusicPlus.com.

Chapter 8: Intermediate Trumpet Techniques

Once we've got those beginner songs down, it might be a good time to branch out into a full, extensive curriculum to further your playing. Let's start with some great, early-instructional books:

Both the "Standard of Excellence" and "Essential Elements" book series for school band are great places to start (although I personally am partial to the Standard of Excellence series through personal experience). Start with book 1 of either set, and both series are color-coded to help you make sure you've snagged the right book; Standard of Excellence's first book contains a red cover, while the first book of the Essential Elements series contains a yellow stripe across the top. They each contain all of the instructional songs listed in the previous chapter, and they are both arranged to gradually stretch out the student and help them grow with songs of gradually-increasing difficulty. They also teach you tidbits along the way, like what "slurs" are (i.e. a stretch of notes where you only 'tongue' the first one, thus resulting in an ultra-smooth passage), or how to recognize a repeat sign. These are typically listed atop the page, and don't ignore them! Too often students will skip over these bits and then not understand how to play fairly basic stuff.

These books will give you plenty of songs to work on that, as mentioned earlier, will incrementally increase both your range and technical prowess simply by playing them. Both books provide a handy fingering chart in the back for every note from the lowest on the trumpet (F♯ below the staff) to top-of-the-staff high G (including all the sharped or flatted pitches). When in doubt, you can write in any fingerings for notes you're unsure how to play on all songs you encounter. They also come with play-along materials so you can make sure you sound good with a full, pre-recorded band. Along the way, if you read the notes atop the pages, they'll teach you how to read, recognize, and play concepts like dynamics, articulation, repeat signs and so on. Pay attention to these! Many new players ignore these tidbits and then have no idea what *mp* means, nor what to do if they see a D.C. al Fine. Since that's often the case, we'll cover some of that here. Heads up, all of these terms will be in Italian.

"Dynamics" is basically a fancy word for "volume." We'll start with the two basic, fundamental poles:

- "Piano", denoted with a *p*, means quiet
- "Forte," denoted with an *f*, means loud

Then, we can get dynamic levels in between those extremes by adding the qualifier "mezzo" *m* to either one. So, we get "mezzo piano" *mp* and "mezzo forte" *mf*. This basically means "somewhat," as in "somewhat quiet." Lastly, we can add even more extreme dynamic values with "fortissimo" and "pianissimo," which mean 'extremely loud' and 'extremely quiet' respectively. We denote these by simply adding an extra *p* or *f* (or even multiple extra dynamic markings!). So, from incredibly quiet to extremely loud, here's the continuum of dynamics:

pp = "pianissimo" (extra quiet)

p = "piano" (quiet)

mp = "mezzo piano" (somewhat quiet)

mf = "mezzo forte" (somewhat loud)

f = "forte" (loud)

ff = "fortissimo" (extra loud)

Dynamics – piano, mezzo piano, mezzo forte, forte, fortissimo

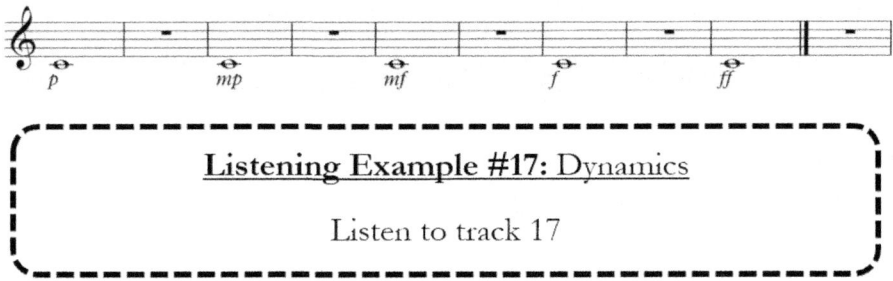

> Listening Example #17: Dynamics
>
> Listen to track 17

Going even further, extra **f**'s or **p**'s can be added for hyperbolic amounts of volume! Next we'll cover repeat signs, which, as the name implies, denote a section of music that the composer wants you to repeat. The dots are in the inside of the repeated section, so a barline that looks like this marks the beginning of a repeating section:

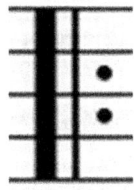

The end of a repeated section is marked with one of these:

Repeated sections can be equipped with "first" and "second endings," as well. These let you know that part of the section is only to be played on the first repetition. The first ending looks like this, and you will need to skip it on the second play-through of the section:

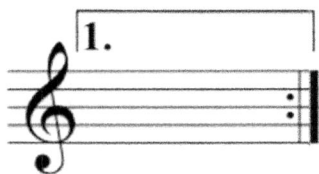

For bigger repeats that cover large chunks of a song, there's "Da Capo" (*D.C.*) and Dal Segno (*D.S.*), which can then end with the song jumping to an entirely different section - the "Coda" - or it can end in the middle of the piece where it says "Fine." Normally, pieces end with the thick, "double barline," which looks like this:

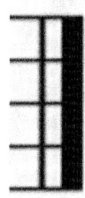

but "Fine" (pronounced "fee-nay," Italian for the end, as in "finish") is used to replace the double barline occasionally.

So, "*D.C. al Fine*" means Da Capo al Fine - which means go back to the very beginning ("Capo" means "head," as in go back to the "top"); then, play until you see "Fine," where the song ends. "*D.S. al Fine*" means the same thing, but instead of going back to the very beginning, simply repeat from the "Segno," or the "sign," which looks like this:

So "D.C." means to repeat from the very beginning, while "D.S." means to repeat from the fancy-looking dollar-sign. Each one can end with "al Coda," meaning "play until you see the 'to Coda' text, and then jump to the separate 'Coda' section." Both the "jump to Coda" instructions and actual Coda section will be marked with this symbol:

This leaves four possible combinations:

- *D.S. al Fine* (go back to the sign, then end where it says "fine")
- *D.S. al Coda* (go back to the sign, then jump to the separate "coda" section from where it says "To Coda")
- *D.C. al Fine* (go back to the beginning, then end where it says "fine")
- *D.C. al Coda* (go back to the beginning, then jump to the separate "coda" section from where it says "To Coda")

Lastly, let's cover accents, staccatos, ties, and slurs.

Now that you've played a few songs on your trumpet and gotten a bit more confident with your sound, it's time to learn a few intermediate techniques. Once you have been practicing for a bit, you may want to learn some more challenging music. When you find more difficult music, there are a few markings and techniques that you will need to know to play it. In this chapter, you will learn more advanced musical notation and a few more advanced techniques to begin practicing on your trumpet.

Articulation

When you first learned to make sounds on the trumpet, you learned about the importance of tonguing. If you remember back from earlier in the book, we discussed that tonguing was a type of articulation. Articulation encompasses many different techniques that designate the attack, strength, and length of notes. Beginning each of the notes with your tongue separates each note from the next, giving it a clear attack and precise sound.

While you will need to tongue (or "articulate") each note in most songs, there are a few instances where you will *not* tongue the notes. One of them is when you see a **slur**. A slur is a curved marking in your music that appears above or below multiple notes.

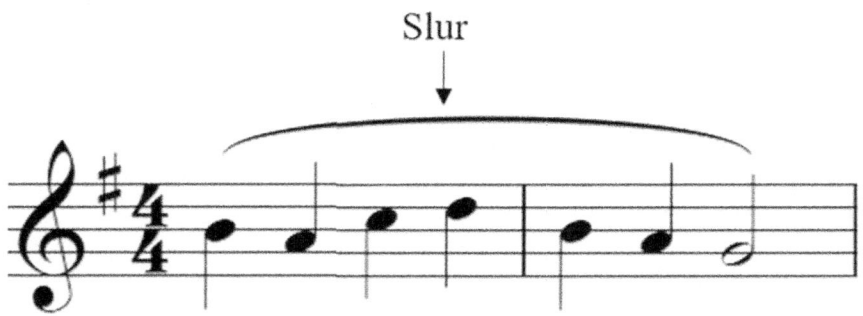

When you see a slur in your music, it means you will not tongue the notes underneath it. You will articulate the first note and continue your air as you move your fingers. Do not stop your air between each note or separate the notes in any way. A slur indicates that this particular section of the music should sound as smooth as possible, with no breaks in the sound for the duration of the slur.

Another marking that looks like a slur is a **tie**. A tie also appears as a curved marking above or below notes - the difference is that a tie appears above two or more notes that are the same. The tie indicates that only the first note should be articulated and your air should continue without separating the notes. Since the notes are the same, it will sound like one long note. In the example below, you will articulate the beginning of your half note and hold the D all the way through the first beat of the next measure.

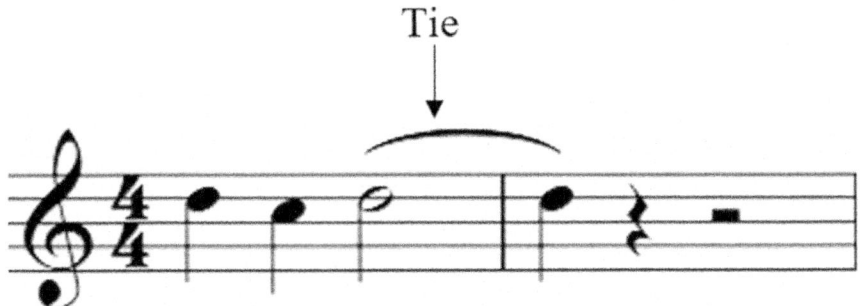

You can differentiate between ties and slurs only by the notes that are underneath the marking. For example:

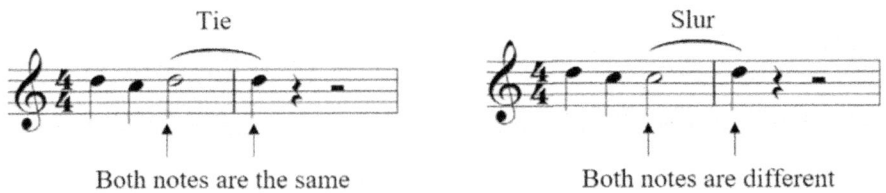

Another articulation marking you may find in intermediate trumpet music is a **tenuto**. A tenuto looks like a small horizontal line on top of or below a note. This tenuto indicates that you should play the note smoothly for its full length. When you see a tenuto marking, it designates that the note or notes over which it appears should be played with a legato style.

When you see a tenuto mark, you will still need to tongue the note, but you will do so delicately with a soft attack on the reed. There should still be a definitive start to the note, but little separation and space. Hold the note(s) out for its full length to ensure there is no break or gap in the sound between notes.

As you may notice, the tenuto can appear above or below the note, depending on the direction of the note's stem. When the stem is pointed up, the tenuto will appear below the note, and when the stem points down, the tenuto appears above the note.

Another articulation marking you may find in intermediate trumpet music is a **staccato**. A staccato mark is a small dot that appears above or below a note. The staccato indicates that you should play each note short and separated. Tonguing is very important in sections of music where staccatos appear. You will want each note to sound crisp and clear, with a hard attack against the reed. The note length will be short – just long enough to make a sound and establish a pitch. There should be space heard between each note in a staccato section.

As you may notice, the staccato can appear above or below the note, depending on the direction of the note's stem. When the stem is pointed up, the staccato will appear below the note, and when the stem points down, the staccato appears above the note.

One final articulation marking that you may find in intermediate music is an **accent**. Accents are a combination of articulation technique and dynamics. They are most commonly found in marches or other strong, emphasized sections of music. An accent looks like a "greater-than" symbol above or below a note (>). It indicates that the note should be brought out and emphasized. To do so, you will need to play accented notes louder, with a strong attack and space between each note.

Tonging is incredibly important for accented notes; you will need a strong, hard attack against the reed. The beginning of each accented note should be clear and emphasized. Accents are used to bring out a certain note or section in the music. Always remember to maintain a controlled sound when playing accented notes – do not overblow or blow so hard that your tone suffers.

These five styles of articulation allow you to play a wide variety of music. Adding in different types of articulation really brings a piece of music to life. Using articulation, you can differentiate between multiple sections of the music, give them each meaning, and begin to play with musicality.

Articulation – slur, legato, staccato

> **Listening Example #18:** Articulations
>
> Listen to tracks 18

Chapter 9: Bringing it all Together

If you'd like to really ramp up your playing another notch, another must-have for any trumpeter is this classic book: Technical Studies for the Cornet by Herbert L. Clarke. You can find this book from any major retailer, be it brick-and-mortar or online, but some kind soul has also uploaded the whole book to the internet in PDF form (link here). The exercises in this book are largely scale-based, building patterns that might be stepwise or arpeggiated, and then feed these patterns through all twelve keys. Complete these exercises and you will know these scales inside and out. If you happen to memorize some of them and incorporate them into your warm-up routine, your fingers will fly like the wind as a result!

> **Listening Example #19:** Technical Studies
>
> Listen to tracks 19

The "first study" is based on the chromatic scale - a fancy word for the 'scale' that includes every single note. It's an ugly, weird, and hard to play scale, although a great one to know. You should definitely do this drill, but actually would recommend starting on the "second study" with #32, as it is based in our key of C and therefore is the easiest.

Another classic technique-builder book is "Arban's Complete Conservatory for Trumpet" (referring to the late legend J.B. Arban). This one is simply massive in terms of number of pages, and as such is a bit more daunting. But, in contains more "etudes," which are short, exercise-like songs. Clarke's book is more filled with exercises, and is therefore more direct and to-the-point. Both are great to have in one's arsenal.

If you have any interest in delving into the world of jazz or pop "standards," there's another book that you should definitely get your hands on: The B♭ "Real" Book. First off, a "standard" is an old-fashioned or traditional pop mega-hit that often predates rock-and-roll - one that's been recorded dozens of times by just as many artists, and despite being a pop song, these often overlap into the world of jazz. For instance "Fly Me to the Moon" would be a classic example, as would any Christmas tune. On that holiday-themed note, "standards" don't *have* to have been released before the rock-and-roll revolution of the 1950s; "All I Want for Christmas is You" definitely would count as a "standard."

The "Real" Book contains the main melody (or "head") to countless standards, as well as the chord changes for improvisational purposes. It's got jazz hits ranging from danceable big band hits to aggressively-difficult bebop cornerstones like "Giant Steps," not to mention pretty much any song Frank Sinatra made famous. Even if most of those don't intrigue you, it's Arban-esque thickness leaves you plenty to choose from (but, since it's all just songs to play and not exercises, you won't feel guilty for skipping over most of the book if you just don't feel like learning those songs).

Beyond that, it might still behoove you to get a private instructor for at least some occasional "drop-in" lessons, so that they can analyze your embouchure, technique, and so on. They can help you pick songs to play that match your skill level while still stretching you out for improvement. Next, some music theory education and ear training would come in handy. MusicTheory.net is a phenomenal resource for self-teaching in both of these fields - it comes with both informative lessons and customizable exercises.

Hopefully this serves as a solid jumping off point for your new adventures in trumpeting! It's by no means an exhaustive game plan for mastery but should get the ball rolling in your endeavor. Happy playing and break a leg out there!

Unlock Your Musical Potential: Get 30% Off the Next Step in Your Instrumental Journey

As a token of appreciation for your dedication, we're excited to offer you an **exclusive 30% discount** on your next product when you sign up below with your email address.

Click the link below:
https://bit.ly/40NikR2
OR
Use the QR Code:

Unlocking your musical potential is easier with ongoing guidance and support. Join our community of passionate musicians to elevate your skills and stay updated with the latest tips and tricks.

By signing up, you'll also receive our periodic newsletter with additional insights and resources to enhance your musical journey.

Your privacy is important to us. We won't spam you, and you can unsubscribe anytime.

Don't miss out on this opportunity to continue your musical journey with this special discount. Sign up now, and let's embark on this musical adventure together!

Printed in Great Britain
by Amazon